Cracking Code o Schizophrenia

Understanding the Symptoms, Causes, and Treatment

By

VIVIAN ANDERSON

Table of contents

Table of contents 3

Chapter 1: Diagnosis of Schizophrenia 3

Chapter 2: Introduction - Schizophrenia and Epigenetics 3

Chapter 3: The Symptoms of Schizophrenia 3

Chapter 4: Risk Factors for Schizophrenia 3

Chapter 5: The Basics of DNA Methylation and Gene Expression ...3

Chapter 6: The Role of DNA Methylation in Schizophrenia 3

Chapter 7: Gene Expression Changes in Schizophrenia 3

Chapter 8: DNA Methylation and Schizophrenia 3

Chapter 9: The Treatment of Schizophrenia through DNA Methylation and Gene Expression 3

Chapter 10: The Role of Psychiatry in Understanding and Treating Schizophrenia 3

Chapter 11: Exploring the Link between DNA Methylation and Schizophrenia: An Overview 3

Chapter 12: Models of Schizophrenia 3
Chapter 13: Psychiatric Treatment for Schizophrenia......................3
Chapter 14: Epigenetic Treatments for Schizophrenia.....................3
Chapter 15: The Role of Cognitive Behavioral Therapy in
Schizophrenia Treatment..3
Chapter 16: Schizophrenia in Children and Adolescents 3
Chapter 17: Schizophrenia and Aging...3
Chapter 18: Schizophrenia and Employment 3
Chapter 19: Living Well with Schizophrenia 3
Chapter 20: The Importance of Social Support in Schizophrenia
Treatment..3
Chapter 21: Supporting Families and Caregivers of People with
Schizophrenia 3
Chapter 22: Addressing Misconceptions about Schizophrenia 3
Chapter 23: Future of Schizophrenia Research 3
Summary..3
Disclaimer..1

Here is a life story of a friend who suffered from schizophrenia and how he managed it.

John was born into a loving family in a small town in the United States. As a child, he was known for his quick wit, outgoing personality, and his love of music. John's parents noticed that he was struggling with his studies in middle school, but they assumed that he was simply bored with the material. However, as John entered high school, his behavior became increasingly erratic. He would have outbursts of anger, speak incoherently, and become fixated on strange ideas. It wasn't until his senior year that John was diagnosed with schizophrenia.

John's diagnosis was devastating for him and his family. He struggled to accept that he had a serious mental illness, and he resisted treatment for several years. During this time, John's behavior became increasingly unpredictable. He dropped out of college, lost his job, and had strained relationships with his friends and family.

It wasn't until John had a particularly severe psychotic episode that he realized he needed help. He was hospitalized for several weeks, and his family worked with his doctors to find the right medication and therapy that would help him manage his symptoms. It was a long road, but John eventually found a combination of medication, cognitive behavioral therapy, and support from his loved ones that allowed him to manage his symptoms and lead a fulfilling life.

John's recovery was not without its challenges. He experienced setbacks, and there were times when he doubted whether he could ever truly overcome his illness. But he persevered, and with the help of his family and healthcare professionals, he gradually gained the skills he needed to manage his condition.

Today, John is an advocate for others living with schizophrenia. He is a member of a support group for people with mental illness, and he regularly speaks at events to raise awareness about the challenges that people with schizophrenia face. John's story is a testament to the fact that with the right treatment and support, people with schizophrenia can lead fulfilling and meaningful lives.

As John continued to manage his condition, he began to explore new interests and hobbies. He rediscovered his love of music and started playing the guitar again, something he had given up during his darkest days. He also found a passion for writing and began to keep a journal where he would reflect on his experiences living with schizophrenia.

Through his journal, John was able to process the difficult emotions that came with his illness. He wrote about the frustration of experiencing delusions and hallucinations, the fear of being judged by others, and the sense of isolation that often comes with mental illness. But he also wrote about the moments of hope and connection that he experienced. He wrote about the joy of spending time with his family, the satisfaction of completing a task, and the comfort he found in his faith.

Over time, John's journal became a powerful tool for him to manage his symptoms. He was able to identify triggers that would cause his symptoms to flare up, and he learned strategies to cope with these challenges. He also found that writing about his experiences helped him to better understand his illness, and to communicate more effectively with his healthcare providers.

As John's confidence grew, he decided to share his writing with others. He submitted some of his work to a local magazine and was thrilled when his essay was published. The response was overwhelmingly positive, and John began to receive messages from other people with mental illness who had been inspired by his story.

Encouraged by this feedback, John began to write more and more. He started a blog, where he would share his experiences and insights about living with schizophrenia. He also began to speak publicly about his illness, sharing his story at mental health conferences and other events.

Today, John is a successful writer and mental health advocate. He has published several books about his experiences with schizophrenia, and he is a sought-after speaker on the topic of mental health. He continues to use his writing as a tool for self-expression and healing, and he is dedicated to helping others who are living with mental illness.

John's story is a powerful reminder that people living with schizophrenia can lead meaningful and fulfilling lives. With the right treatment, support, and self-care strategies, it is possible to manage this challenging condition and thrive despite its many obstacles.

Chapter 1: Diagnosis of Schizophrenia

Diagnosing schizophrenia can be a complex process, as the disorder shares symptoms with other mental health conditions such as bipolar disorder and major depressive disorder. To diagnose schizophrenia, mental health professionals typically use a combination of approaches, including:

1. Clinical interviews: Mental health professionals will typically conduct an in-depth clinical interview to assess a person's symptoms and medical history. This may involve questions about the person's thoughts, feelings, behaviors, and experiences.

2. Diagnostic criteria: Mental health professionals will typically use diagnostic criteria from the Diagnostic and Statistical Manual of Mental Disorders (DSM-5) to assess a person's symptoms and determine if they fit the requirements for a schizophrenia diagnosis.

3. Psychiatric evaluation: A psychiatric evaluation may involve additional tests or assessments, such as psychological testing, to further evaluate a person's symptoms and mental health.

A person must have at least two of the following symptoms for a sufficient amount of time over the course of one month in order to be diagnosed with schizophrenia:

1. Delusions: False beliefs that are not based in reality, such as believing that one is being followed or controlled by others.

2. Hallucinations: Sensory experiences that are not based on reality, such as hearing voices or seeing things that are not there.

3. Disorganized speech: Speech that is difficult to follow or understand, with the frequent derailment, incoherence, or loose associations.

4. Grossly disorganized or catatonic behavior: Abnormal movements or behaviors, such as pacing, rocking, or rigid immobility.

5. Negative symptoms: A lack of emotional expression or motivation, including reduced speech, flattened affect, or lack of interest in social activities.

In addition to experiencing these symptoms, a person must also experience significant impairment in their ability to function at work, school, or in other areas of life.

It is important to note that while a diagnosis of schizophrenia can be difficult, it is also important for effective treatment and management of the disorder. In the next chapter, we will explore the different treatment options available for people with schizophrenia.

Chapter 2: Introduction - Schizophrenia and Epigenetics

Schizophrenia is a severe and chronic mental illness that affects how a person thinks, feels, and behaves, it affects approximately 1% of the population worldwide. It is a complex condition that arises from a combination of genetic and environmental factors. While the exact cause of schizophrenia remains unknown, recent research has shown that epigenetic modifications, such as DNA methylation and gene expression, may play a key role in its development and progression.

The field of epigenetics studies heritable variations in gene expression that do not result from changes to the underlying DNA sequence. Epigenetic modifications, such as DNA methylation and histone modification, can change the way that genes are expressed, turning them on or off, and thus altering the function of cells and tissues. These changes can occur in response to environmental factors, such as diet, stress, and exposure to toxins, as well as during development and aging.

Over the past decade, a growing body of research has investigated the role of epigenetics in schizophrenia. Studies have identified epigenetic changes in several genes and pathways associated with the disorder, including genes involved in neurotransmitter signaling, synaptic plasticity, and immune system function.

One area of particular interest has been DNA methylation, which involves the addition of a methyl group to a cytosine base in DNA. DNA methylation can silence gene expression by blocking the binding of transcription factors and other regulatory proteins to the DNA sequence. Aberrant DNA methylation has been implicated in several psychiatric disorders, including schizophrenia, and has been linked to changes in brain function and behavior.

A number of studies have reported altered DNA methylation patterns in patients with schizophrenia, as well as in their relatives and in individuals with a high genetic risk for the disorder. For example, a study published in the American Journal of Psychiatry in 2014 found that DNA methylation levels were significantly altered in several genes involved in immune system function in patients with schizophrenia. Another study published in Biological Psychiatry in 2018 identified differential DNA methylation patterns in the brain tissue of patients with schizophrenia compared to healthy controls.

In addition to DNA methylation, research has also investigated the role of gene expression in schizophrenia.

Gene expression refers to the process by which genetic information is converted into functional proteins or RNA molecules. Altered gene expression can result in changes in cellular function and has been implicated in several neuropsychiatric disorders, including schizophrenia.

Several studies have identified changes in gene expression in patients with schizophrenia, including genes involved in synaptic plasticity, neurotransmitter signaling, and immune system function. For example, a study published in Nature in 2016 identified differential gene expression patterns in the prefrontal cortex of patients with schizophrenia compared to healthy controls. Another study published in Schizophrenia Research in 2018 found that genes involved in synaptic function and neurodevelopment were differentially expressed in the brains of individuals with schizophrenia.

While the exact mechanisms by which DNA methylation and gene expression alterations contribute to schizophrenia are still not fully understood, research has suggested that they may play a role in disrupting neural circuitry and synaptic plasticity in the brain. In addition, epigenetic modifications may interact with environmental factors, such as stress and substance abuse, to increase the risk of developing schizophrenia.

Despite the advances in our understanding of the role of

epigenetics in schizophrenia, much work remains to be done. Future research will need to address a number of key questions, such as how epigenetic modifications interact with genetic and environmental factors to contribute to the disorder, and how these modifications can be targeted for therapeutic intervention.

Schizophrenia affects approximately 1% of the global population, and its symptoms can include hallucinations, delusions, disorganized thinking and speech, and decreased emotional expression. The disorder typically develops in late adolescence or early adulthood and is often chronic, with a significant impact on a person's daily functioning and quality of life.

While genetic factors have long been known to play a role in the development of schizophrenia, the complex nature of the disorder has made it difficult to identify specific genes and genetic variations involved. Epigenetics offers a promising avenue for understanding the biological mechanisms underlying schizophrenia and may provide new insights into potential treatments.

Epigenetic modifications can be influenced by a range of environmental factors, including prenatal stress, early life experiences, diet, and exposure to toxins. For example, studies have shown that maternal stress during pregnancy can lead to epigenetic changes in the developing fetus that increase the risk of schizophrenia and other psychiatric disorders.

In addition to DNA methylation and gene expression, other epigenetic modifications have also been implicated in schizophrenia. These include changes in histone modifications, non-coding RNA, and chromatin structure. The study of epigenetics in schizophrenia is a rapidly evolving field, with new findings and technologies continually emerging.

One promising area of research involves the use of epigenetic biomarkers for predicting and diagnosing schizophrenia. Several studies have reported epigenetic changes that are specific to the disorder and can be detected in blood or other tissues. These biomarkers could potentially be used to identify individuals at high risk for developing schizophrenia or to monitor treatment response.

Another area of research involves the development of epigenetic therapies for schizophrenia. While traditional pharmacological treatments for schizophrenia primarily target neurotransmitter systems, epigenetic therapies could provide a more targeted approach to treating the underlying biological mechanisms of the disorder. For example, drugs that target DNA methylation or histone modifications have shown promise in preclinical studies.

Chapter 3: The Symptoms of Schizophrenia

Schizophrenia is a complex and multifaceted disorder, and its symptoms can vary widely from person to person. However, there are a number of common symptoms that are associated with the disorder. These symptoms are classified into three types: positive symptoms, negative symptoms, and cognitive symptoms.

Positive Symptoms

Positive symptoms are experiences or behaviors that are added to a person's mental state and are not present in healthy individuals. These symptoms are often the most noticeable and are typically what first bring individuals with schizophrenia to the attention of mental health professionals. Some common positive symptoms include:

1. Hallucinations: This is when a person experiences sensory perceptions that are not based on reality. The most common hallucinations associated with schizophrenia are auditory, such as hearing voices that are not there.

2. Delusions: This is when a person holds onto beliefs that are not based on reality. Delusions can take many forms, but some common types include beliefs that one is being persecuted, that one has special

powers, or that one's thoughts are being broadcast to others.

3. Disorganized thinking: This is when a person has difficulty organizing their thoughts and making sense of information. This can lead to speech that is difficult to follow or understand.

Negative Symptoms

Negative symptoms are experiences or behaviors that are removed from a person's mental state and are present in healthy individuals. These symptoms are often more subtle and can be harder to detect than positive symptoms. Some common negative symptoms include:

1. Lack of motivation: This is when a person has difficulty finding the energy or drive to engage in activities they once enjoyed or to complete tasks.

2. Social withdrawal: This is when a person becomes less interested in socializing with others and may become isolated.

3. Blunted affect: This is when a person shows little emotional expression and may appear flat or unresponsive.

Cognitive Symptoms

Cognitive symptoms are difficulties with thinking, learning, and memory that are often associated with schizophrenia. These symptoms can be a significant source of impairment for individuals with the disorder, as they can affect daily functioning and the ability to work or attend school. Some common cognitive symptoms include:

1. Difficulty with attention: This is when a person has difficulty focusing their attention and may become easily distracted.

2. Memory problems: This is when a person has difficulty remembering information or experiences.

3. Executive functioning deficits: This is when a person has difficulty with planning, decision-making, and other higher-level cognitive processes.

Chapter 4: Risk Factors for Schizophrenia

Schizophrenia is a complex disorder that is influenced by a variety of factors. While the exact causes of the disorder are not yet fully understood, researchers have identified several risk factors that may contribute to the development of schizophrenia. These risk factors include:

1. Genetics: There is strong evidence that genetics plays a role in the development of schizophrenia. People who have a family history of the disorder are at increased risk of developing it themselves.

2. Environmental factors: Exposure to certain environmental factors, such as infection, malnutrition, or substance abuse, during pregnancy or early childhood may increase the risk of developing schizophrenia later in life.

3. Brain development: Schizophrenia is thought to be associated with abnormal brain development, particularly in the prefrontal cortex and hippocampus. Factors that disrupt normal brain development, such as prenatal exposure to toxins, may increase the risk of developing the disorder.

4. Substance abuse: Substance abuse, particularly the use of cannabis, has been associated with an increased risk of developing schizophrenia. This is thought to be due to the impact of substances on brain development and function.

5. Stressful life events: Exposure to stressful life events, such as trauma or loss, may increase the risk of developing schizophrenia. Stress has been shown to impact brain development and function, and may contribute to the development of the disorder.

It is important to note that while these risk factors are associated with an increased risk of developing schizophrenia, they do not necessarily cause the disorder. Many people who have these risk factors do not go on to develop schizophrenia, and many people who develop the disorder do not have a clear history of these risk factors.

Chapter 5: The Basics of DNA Methylation and Gene Expression

In this chapter, we will explore the basic concepts of DNA methylation and gene expression and their role in regulating gene activity.

DNA Methylation:

DNA methylation is a process by which a methyl group (CH3) is added to the cytosine nucleotide of DNA. This modification is catalyzed by enzymes known as DNA methyltransferases (DNMTs). Methylation typically occurs on cytosines that are adjacent to guanines, a pattern known as CpG dinucleotides.

DNA methylation is an important epigenetic mechanism that plays a crucial role in regulating gene expression. Methylation of promoter regions of genes can prevent the binding of transcription factors, which are proteins that regulate gene expression, thereby silencing gene activity. In contrast, methylation of enhancer regions can promote the binding of transcription factors, leading to increased gene expression.

The process of DNA methylation is dynamic and can be influenced by a range of environmental factors. For example, exposure to stress or toxins can lead to changes in DNA methylation patterns, which can have long-lasting effects on gene expression.

Gene Expression:

Gene expression refers to the process by which the genetic information encoded in DNA is used to produce proteins, the building blocks of cells. Gene expression is regulated by a complex network of factors, including transcription factors, RNA polymerase, and various epigenetic modifications.

Transcription is the first step in gene expression and involves the production of messenger RNA (mRNA) from DNA. Transcription factors bind to specific regions of DNA, known as enhancers or promoters, and recruit RNA polymerase, which synthesizes the mRNA molecule.

After transcription, mRNA is processed and transported out of the nucleus and into the cytoplasm, where it is translated into protein by ribosomes. The rate of translation can also be regulated by various factors, including microRNAs, which are small RNA molecules that can bind to mRNA and prevent translation.

The regulation of gene expression is a complex process that is influenced by a wide range of factors, including epigenetic modifications such as DNA methylation and histone modifications. Dysregulation of gene expression can lead to a range of diseases and disorders, including cancer and neurological disorders such as schizophrenia.

The Role of DNA Methylation and Gene Expression in Schizophrenia:

Studies have shown that DNA methylation and gene expression play important roles in the development and progression of schizophrenia. For example, several genes that are known to be involved in neurotransmitter signaling and brain development have been found to be differentially expressed in individuals with schizophrenia.

In addition, several studies have reported altered DNA methylation patterns in individuals with schizophrenia, particularly in genes involved in neurodevelopment and synaptic function. These findings suggest that epigenetic dysregulation may contribute to the development of the disorder.

Furthermore, environmental factors such as prenatal stress and exposure to toxins have been shown to alter DNA methylation patterns and gene expression, which could increase the risk of developing schizophrenia.

In addition to genetic and epigenetic factors, environmental factors such as early life stress, infections, and drug abuse have also been implicated in the development of schizophrenia. These environmental factors may interact with genetic and epigenetic factors to alter brain development and function, ultimately leading to the development of the disorder.

One proposed mechanism by which environmental factors may influence gene expression is through changes in DNA methylation patterns. For example, a study found that individuals who experienced childhood trauma had altered DNA methylation patterns in several genes involved in stress response, which could increase the risk of developing psychiatric disorders such as schizophrenia.

Another study found that prenatal exposure to the influenza virus was associated with altered DNA methylation patterns in genes involved in neurodevelopment and immune function. These changes in DNA methylation could disrupt normal brain development, leading to an increased risk of developing schizophrenia.

Understanding the complex interactions between genetic, epigenetic, and environmental factors in the development of schizophrenia is a major challenge facing researchers in the field. However, recent advances in technology and computational methods have provided new tools for investigating these complex interactions.

For example, genome-wide association studies (GWAS) have identified several genetic variants that are associated with an increased risk of schizophrenia. However, the vast majority of these variants are located in non-coding regions of the genome, which suggests that they may be involved in regulating gene expression rather than coding for proteins.

To identify the specific genes and pathways that are dysregulated in schizophrenia, researchers have begun to use transcriptomics, a technique that allows them to measure the expression of all genes in a cell or tissue at once. By comparing the transcriptomes of individuals with schizophrenia to those of healthy individuals, researchers can identify genes that are differentially expressed in the disorder and begin to unravel the complex molecular pathways that underlie the disorder.

Chapter 6: The Role of DNA Methylation in Schizophrenia

DNA methylation is a key epigenetic mechanism that regulates gene expression in many biological processes. It involves the addition of a methyl group to the cytosine base of DNA, which can lead to the silencing of gene expression. In recent years, there has been increasing evidence to suggest that DNA methylation plays a role in the development of schizophrenia.

One study found that individuals with schizophrenia have altered DNA methylation patterns in several genes involved in neurodevelopment and synaptic plasticity. These changes in DNA methylation may disrupt normal brain development and function, leading to the development of the disorder.

Another study found that prenatal exposure to the antipsychotic drug valproic acid, which is known to disrupt DNA methylation, was associated with an increased risk of schizophrenia in offspring. This shows that abnormalities in DNA methylation during early development may have a role in the disorder's development.

In addition, several genetic variants associated with an increased risk of schizophrenia have been found to be located in or near genes involved in DNA methylation. This suggests that disruptions in DNA methylation may be an important mechanism by which these genetic variants contribute to the development of the disorder.

However, the exact mechanisms by which alterations in DNA methylation contribute to the development of schizophrenia are not yet fully understood. It is possible that disruptions in DNA methylation may lead to alterations in gene expression that ultimately result in the development of the disorder. Alternatively, alterations in DNA methylation may reflect underlying changes in chromatin structure or other epigenetic modifications that contribute to the development of the disorder.

Despite these uncertainties, recent studies have begun to shed light on the specific genes and pathways that are dysregulated in schizophrenia as a result of alterations in DNA methylation. For example, one study found that alterations in DNA methylation in a gene called GAD1 were associated with a decrease in the expression of this gene in the brains of individuals with schizophrenia. GAD1 is involved in the synthesis of the neurotransmitter GABA, which is known to be disrupted in schizophrenia.

Another study found that alterations in DNA methylation in a gene called BDNF were associated with a decrease in the expression of this gene in the brains of individuals with schizophrenia. BDNF is involved in the growth and survival of neurons, and alterations in its expression have been implicated in several psychiatric disorders.

Chapter 7: Gene Expression Changes in Schizophrenia

Gene expression is the process by which information stored in DNA is used to produce proteins that carry out various functions in the body. In recent years, there has been growing evidence to suggest that changes in gene expression may play a role in the development of schizophrenia.

One study found that individuals with schizophrenia have alterations in the expression of several genes involved in neurodevelopment and synaptic function. Specifically, these individuals had decreased expression of genes involved in synaptic transmission and increased expression of genes involved in immune response and inflammation. These changes in gene expression may contribute to the cognitive and behavioral symptoms of schizophrenia.

Another study found that changes in the expression of genes involved in GABA neurotransmission were associated with the development of schizophrenia. GABA is an inhibitory neurotransmitter that aids in the regulation of other neurotransmitter activities in the brain. Disruptions in GABA neurotransmission have been implicated in several psychiatric disorders, including schizophrenia.

In addition, several genetic variants associated with an increased risk of schizophrenia have been found to be located in or near genes involved in gene expression. This suggests that disruptions in gene expression may be an important mechanism by which these genetic variants contribute to the development of the disorder.

Recent studies have also begun to identify specific molecular pathways that are dysregulated in schizophrenia as a result of changes in gene expression. For example, one study found that the Wnt signaling pathway, which is involved in neurodevelopment and synaptic function, was dysregulated in individuals with schizophrenia. This dysregulation may contribute to the cognitive and behavioral symptoms of the disorder.

Another study found that alterations in the expression of genes involved in mitochondrial function were associated with the development of schizophrenia. Organelles called mitochondria are found in cells and are in charge of generating energy.

Disruptions in mitochondrial function have been implicated in several psychiatric disorders, including schizophrenia.

Despite these advances, the exact mechanisms by which changes in gene expression contribute to the development of schizophrenia are not yet fully understood. It is possible that changes in gene expression may lead to alterations in protein function that ultimately result in the development of the disorder. Alternatively, changes in gene expression may reflect underlying changes in chromatin structure or other epigenetic modifications that contribute to the development of the disorder.

Chapter 8: DNA Methylation and Schizophrenia

Schizophrenia is a complex neuropsychiatric disorder that affects approximately 1% of the population worldwide. While genetic factors have long been known to play a role in the development of schizophrenia, recent research has suggested that epigenetic mechanisms, including DNA methylation, may also contribute to the disorder.

DNA methylation is an epigenetic modification that involves the addition of a methyl group to cytosine residues in DNA, typically in the context of a CpG dinucleotide. Methylation of CpG islands in promoter regions of genes is associated with decreased gene expression, while methylation of gene bodies may enhance transcriptional elongation.

Several studies have identified differential DNA methylation patterns in the brains of individuals with schizophrenia compared to healthy controls. For example, a study using post-mortem brain tissue found that DNA methylation levels in the promoter region of the gene for brain-derived neurotrophic factor (BDNF) were lower in individuals with schizophrenia compared to controls. BDNF is a neurotrophic factor involved in the growth and survival of neurons and has been implicated in the development of schizophrenia.

Another study found that DNA methylation of the gene for reelin, a protein involved in neuronal migration and synaptic plasticity, was decreased in the prefrontal cortex of individuals with schizophrenia compared to controls. Additionally, a genome-wide association study (GWAS) identified several single-nucleotide polymorphisms (SNPs) in genes involved in DNA methylation that were associated with increased risk for schizophrenia.

While these studies provide strong evidence for an association between DNA methylation and schizophrenia, the underlying mechanisms by which alterations in DNA methylation contribute to the disorder are still not fully understood. One possibility is that changes in DNA methylation alter gene expression in key pathways involved in the development and function of the brain.

Several candidate genes and pathways have been identified that may be affected by alterations in DNA methylation in schizophrenia. For example, the dopamine receptor D2 gene (DRD2) has been implicated in the pathophysiology of schizophrenia and has been shown to be regulated by DNA methylation. Other genes involved in synaptic plasticity and neuronal development, such as neuregulin 1 (NRG1) and the glutamate receptor subunit 3 (GRIA3), have also been found to be differentially methylated in individuals with schizophrenia.

In addition to its potential as a biomarker for schizophrenia, DNA methylation may also have therapeutic implications. Recent studies have shown that targeting DNA methylation with drugs such as DNMT inhibitors can improve cognitive and behavioral symptoms in animal models of schizophrenia.

However, the use of DNMT inhibitors in humans is still in its early stages and further research is needed to determine their safety and efficacy in treating schizophrenia. Additionally, it is important to consider the potential long-term effects of altering DNA methylation, as it may have unintended consequences on gene expression and other epigenetic modifications.

Moreover, the complexity of epigenetic regulation in the brain suggests that DNA methylation may be only one piece of a larger puzzle in understanding the development of schizophrenia. Other epigenetic modifications, such as histone modifications and non-coding RNA, may also play important roles in the regulation of gene expression in the brain.

One promising avenue of research is the use of epigenome-wide association studies (EWAS) to identify specific epigenetic modifications associated with schizophrenia. By analyzing DNA methylation and other epigenetic marks across the entire genome, these studies may provide a more comprehensive understanding of the epigenetic changes that occur in the brains of individuals with schizophrenia.

Chapter 9: The Treatment of Schizophrenia through DNA Methylation and Gene Expression

Schizophrenia is a complex mental illness that affects millions of people around the world. It is a chronic condition that can significantly impact an individual's quality of life. While there is no cure for schizophrenia, various treatments can help manage its symptoms and improve the patient's overall well-being. In recent years, researchers have investigated the role of DNA methylation and gene expression in the development and progression of schizophrenia. This chapter explores the potential of using DNA methylation and gene expression as a treatment for schizophrenia.

The treatment of schizophrenia can be challenging, and it often requires a combination of medication and psychotherapy. However, the efficacy of these treatments varies among individuals, and some patients may not respond to them at all. This has led researchers to investigate alternative treatment approaches, such as using DNA methylation and gene expression.

One potential treatment approach for schizophrenia is DNA methylation. DNA methylation is a process that involves the addition of a methyl group to DNA molecules, which can affect gene expression. In individuals with schizophrenia, specific genes may be overexpressed or underexpressed, leading to abnormal brain function. By targeting these genes through DNA methylation, it may be possible to restore normal gene expression and improve brain function in individuals with schizophrenia.

Another potential treatment approach is gene expression. Gene expression refers to the process of turning a gene on or off. Abnormal gene expression has been linked to a range of mental disorders, including schizophrenia. Researchers have identified several genes that are associated with schizophrenia, and by modulating their expression, it may be possible to improve the symptoms of the disorder.

One way to modulate gene expression is through the use of drugs that target specific genes. Drugs that target the dopamine receptor, for example, have been used to treat schizophrenia. Dopamine is a neurotransmitter that plays a role in regulating mood and behavior, and abnormalities in its function have been linked to schizophrenia. By targeting the dopamine receptor, it may be possible to improve the symptoms of the disorder.

Another way to modulate gene expression is through the use of non-drug interventions. For example, transcranial magnetic stimulation (TMS) is a non-invasive procedure that uses magnetic fields to stimulate specific regions of the brain. TMS has been used to treat a range of mental disorders, including depression and schizophrenia. By stimulating specific regions of the brain, it may be possible to modulate gene expression and improve the symptoms of the disorder.

While DNA methylation and gene expression hold promise as potential treatments for schizophrenia, further research is needed to determine their efficacy and safety. Additionally, these treatments may not be suitable for all patients with schizophrenia, and their use may be limited to specific subgroups of patients. Nonetheless, the potential of using DNA methylation and gene expression as treatments for schizophrenia highlights the need for continued research into the underlying causes of the disorder.

The results of these studies highlight the need for continued research into the mechanisms underlying DNA methylation changes and gene expression in schizophrenia. Further investigation into the specific genes affected by DNA methylation and the downstream effects on protein expression and brain function may help to elucidate the molecular mechanisms involved in the development and progression of schizophrenia.

Additionally, there is a growing interest in the potential therapeutic implications of targeting DNA methylation and gene expression in the treatment of schizophrenia. Several preclinical studies have demonstrated the potential of epigenetic-targeted therapies, such as DNA methyltransferase inhibitors, in improving cognitive function and ameliorating symptoms of schizophrenia in animal models.

While these findings are promising, further research is needed to fully understand the safety and efficacy of these treatments in humans. Clinical trials investigating the effects of DNA methyltransferase inhibitors and other epigenetic-targeted therapies on schizophrenia patients are currently ongoing, and their results may have important implications for the future of schizophrenia treatment.

Chapter 10: The Role of Psychiatry in Understanding and Treating Schizophrenia

Schizophrenia is a complex and debilitating mental disorder that affects millions of people worldwide. While significant progress has been made in understanding the genetic and epigenetic factors that contribute to the development and progression of the disorder, the role of psychiatry in diagnosing and treating schizophrenia remains crucial.

Psychiatry is the branch of medicine that focuses on the diagnosis, treatment, and prevention of mental illness, including schizophrenia. Psychiatrists are medical doctors who specialize in mental health and are trained to diagnose and treat a wide range of mental disorders.

The diagnosis of schizophrenia is based on the presence of specific symptoms, such as delusions, hallucinations, disorganized speech, and disorganized behavior. These symptoms can significantly impair a person's ability to function in daily life and may require hospitalization in severe cases.

Psychiatrists use a combination of clinical interviews, physical examinations, and laboratory tests to diagnose schizophrenia. The Diagnostic and Statistical Manual of Mental Disorders, Fifth Edition (DSM-5) is the primary diagnostic tool used by psychiatrists to diagnose mental disorders, including schizophrenia. The DSM-5 outlines specific diagnostic criteria for schizophrenia based on the presence of specific symptoms.

Once a diagnosis of schizophrenia is made, psychiatrists work with patients to develop a treatment plan tailored to their individual needs. The treatment of schizophrenia typically involves a combination of medications and psychotherapy.

Antipsychotic medications are the cornerstone of schizophrenia treatment and are used to reduce the severity of symptoms such as delusions and hallucinations. These medications work by blocking the action of dopamine, a neurotransmitter that is believed to be involved in the development of schizophrenia.

Psychotherapy, such as cognitive-behavioral therapy (CBT) and family therapy, is also an important component of schizophrenia treatment. CBT helps patients to identify and challenge negative thought patterns and beliefs that contribute to the development of symptoms, while family therapy can help to improve communication and relationships within the patient's support system.

In addition to medication and psychotherapy, other interventions may be used to treat specific symptoms of schizophrenia. For example, occupational therapy can help patients to develop the skills needed to perform daily activities, while social skills training can help patients to improve their communication and interpersonal skills.

The treatment of schizophrenia requires ongoing monitoring and adjustment to ensure that patients are receiving the most effective care. Psychiatrists work closely with patients to monitor their symptoms and adjust their treatment plans as needed to ensure that they are receiving the best possible care.

In recent years, there has been a growing interest in the potential of early intervention in the treatment of schizophrenia. Early intervention involves identifying and treating the disorder as soon as possible after the onset of symptoms, with the goal of improving long-term outcomes and reducing the severity of symptoms.

Early intervention in the treatment of schizophrenia may involve a combination of medication, psychotherapy, and psychosocial interventions. For example, programs such as coordinated specialty care (CSC) have been developed to provide a comprehensive, team-based approach to the treatment of early psychosis.

The role of psychiatry in understanding and treating schizophrenia is essential to improving the lives of people affected by the disorder. With advances in diagnosis and treatment, patients with schizophrenia can lead fulfilling lives with the appropriate care and support.

Chapter 11: Exploring the Link between DNA Methylation and

Schizophrenia: An Overview

Schizophrenia is a complex mental disorder that affects millions of people around the world. While the exact causes of schizophrenia are not fully understood, researchers believe that genetics plays a significant role in its development.

Recent studies have shown that DNA methylation, a process that regulates gene expression, may be linked to the development of schizophrenia. DNA methylation is a chemical modification that occurs when a methyl group is added to a cytosine residue in the DNA molecule. This process can affect the way genes are expressed, either by increasing or decreasing their activity.

In individuals with schizophrenia, researchers have observed changes in DNA methylation patterns in certain regions of the genome. Specifically, they have found increased methylation in genes associated with neurotransmitter signaling, neuronal development, and immune function.

These findings suggest that abnormal DNA methylation may disrupt the proper functioning of the brain and contribute to the development of schizophrenia. However, researchers are still working to understand the exact mechanisms by which DNA methylation influences the development of this complex disorder.

One possibility is that DNA methylation may affect the expression of genes involved in dopamine signaling, a process that is known to be disrupted in individuals with schizophrenia. Dopamine is a neurotransmitter that plays a critical role in regulating mood, motivation, and movement, among other functions. Other studies have suggested that abnormal DNA methylation may affect the expression of genes involved in neuronal development and synaptic plasticity, processes that are essential for the proper functioning of the brain. Disruptions in these processes have been linked to a range of neurological and psychiatric disorders, including schizophrenia.

Despite these promising findings, there is still much that researchers do not know about the relationship between DNA methylation and schizophrenia. For example, it is unclear whether changes in DNA methylation patterns are a cause or a consequence of the disorder. Additionally, it is not yet clear whether these changes are specific to schizophrenia or if they are also present in other psychiatric disorders.

Moving forward, researchers will need to continue investigating the link between DNA methylation and schizophrenia in order to gain a better understanding of this complex disorder. By unraveling the genetic and epigenetic mechanisms that contribute to the development of schizophrenia, researchers may be able to develop more effective treatments and interventions for this devastating condition.

Chapter 12: Models of Schizophrenia

While studying humans with schizophrenia is crucial, animal models of schizophrenia can provide researchers with an additional means of understanding the disorder. Animal models of schizophrenia are created by manipulating certain genes or environmental factors in animals to produce symptoms similar to those found in human patients. By studying these animal models, researchers can better understand the underlying biological mechanisms of schizophrenia and develop potential treatments.

1. Types of Animal Models

There are several types of animal models used in schizophrenia research, including pharmacological models, lesion models, and genetic models. Pharmacological models involve administering drugs that produce schizophrenia-like symptoms in animals, while lesion models involve damaging specific brain regions to produce similar symptoms. Genetic models are created by selectively breeding animals with genes that are associated with schizophrenia in humans.

2. Advantages of Animal Models

Animal models have several advantages in schizophrenia research. First, they allow researchers to study the disease in a controlled environment, which is not always possible in human studies. Second, animal models can be used to test potential treatments before they are given to human patients. Third, animal models can provide insights into the basic biological mechanisms of the disorder.

3. Limitations of Animal Models

However, there are also several limitations to using animal models in schizophrenia research. One limitation is that animals cannot report subjective experiences, such as hallucinations or delusions. Additionally, animal models may not fully capture the complexity of the disorder in humans, as the animals may not exhibit all of the same symptoms as human patients. Finally, animal models may not accurately reflect the genetic and environmental factors that contribute to the disorder in humans.

4. Examples of Animal Models

Several animal models have been used in schizophrenia research. For example, the neonatal ventral hippocampal lesion (NVHL) model involves lesioning the ventral hippocampus in rats shortly after birth, which produces several schizophrenia-like symptoms, including social withdrawal and cognitive deficits. Another example is the DISC1 mouse model, which involves altering the DISC1 gene in mice, a gene that has been linked to schizophrenia in humans. These mice exhibit several schizophrenia-like symptoms, including impaired spatial working memory and deficits in sociability.

5. The Importance of Animal Models
Despite their limitations, animal models are an important tool in schizophrenia research. They allow researchers to investigate the underlying biology of the disorder and test potential treatments in a controlled environment. By combining animal models with human studies, researchers can gain a more comprehensive understanding of the disorder and work towards developing better treatments for those who suffer from schizophrenia.

Chapter 13: Psychiatric Treatment for Schizophrenia

Schizophrenia is a complex mental illness that requires careful and comprehensive treatment. There is no known cure for schizophrenia, but with the right combination of medications, therapy, and support, many people with this disorder can lead fulfilling lives. This chapter will discuss the different types of treatments available for schizophrenia.

Medications are the most common treatment for schizophrenia. Symptoms such as delusions, hallucinations, and disorganized thinking can be helped by antipsychotic medicines. These medications work by blocking dopamine receptors in the brain, which can reduce the levels of this neurotransmitter that is believed to play a role in the development of schizophrenia.

There are two types of antipsychotic medications: typical and atypical. Typical antipsychotics are the older generation of medications and tend to cause more side effects. Atypical antipsychotics are newer medications and tend to have fewer side effects, although they can still cause weight gain and other problems.

In addition to medications, therapy can be helpful for people with schizophrenia. Cognitive-behavioral therapy (CBT) is a type of therapy that focuses on changing thought patterns and behaviors that contribute to symptoms of schizophrenia. CBT can help people with schizophrenia learn coping skills and develop strategies for managing their symptoms.

Family therapy can also be helpful for people with schizophrenia. Family therapy can help family members better understand the illness and learn how to provide support to their loved ones. It can also help improve communication within the family and reduce stress.

Another important aspect of treatment for schizophrenia is support. Support groups can provide a sense of community and belonging for people with schizophrenia, as well as a safe space to discuss their experiences and challenges. Peer support groups, where people with schizophrenia support each other, can be particularly beneficial.

Recovery from schizophrenia is a lifelong process, and it is important to have ongoing support and treatment. In addition to medications, therapy, and support groups, other treatments such as vocational rehabilitation and housing assistance may be helpful for people with schizophrenia.

Vocational rehabilitation can help people with schizophrenia find and maintain employment. This can be an important part of recovery, as it can provide a sense of purpose and improve self-esteem. Housing assistance can also be important, as stable housing can reduce stress and provide a safe and supportive environment.

Chapter 14: Epigenetic Treatments for Schizophrenia

Epigenetics is a rapidly growing field that has the potential to revolutionize the treatment of schizophrenia. Epigenetic modifications, such as DNA methylation and histone modifications, can alter gene expression without changing the underlying DNA sequence. In recent years, researchers have begun to explore the potential of epigenetic therapies for treating schizophrenia.

1. The Promise of Epigenetic Therapies

Epigenetic therapies for schizophrenia aim to restore normal gene expression patterns by targeting the specific epigenetic modifications that are associated with the disorder. This approach has several advantages over traditional drug therapies, which often have limited efficacy and can produce unwanted side effects.

2. Current Epigenetic Therapies

Several epigenetic therapies are currently being investigated for the treatment of schizophrenia. For example, the histone deacetylase (HDAC) inhibitor valproic acid has been shown to improve symptoms in animal models of schizophrenia by increasing histone acetylation and altering gene expression. Other HDAC inhibitors, such as sodium butyrate and trichostatin A, have also shown promise in preclinical studies.

In addition to HDAC inhibitors, DNA methyltransferase (DNMT) inhibitors are also being explored as potential treatments for schizophrenia. DNMT inhibitors work by blocking the enzyme responsible for DNA methylation, which can restore normal gene expression patterns. The DNMT inhibitor zebularine has shown efficacy in animal models of schizophrenia by improving cognitive function and reducing dopamine-related behaviors.

3. Challenges of Epigenetic Therapies

Despite their promise, there are several challenges associated with developing epigenetic therapies for schizophrenia. One challenge is the need to develop therapies that are specific to the epigenetic modifications that are associated with the disorder. Additionally, the long-term safety and efficacy of epigenetic therapies are not yet fully understood.

4. Future Directions

Despite these challenges, the potential of epigenetic therapies for schizophrenia is significant. As researchers continue to explore the underlying epigenetic mechanisms of the disorder, they may identify new targets for therapy. In the future, it is possible that epigenetic therapies will become an important tool in the treatment of schizophrenia, offering patients a safer and more effective alternative to traditional drug therapies.

Overall, epigenetic therapies hold great promise for the treatment of schizophrenia. By targeting the specific epigenetic modifications that are associated with the disorder, researchers may be able to restore normal gene expression patterns and improve symptoms in patients. However, further research is needed to fully understand the potential of epigenetic therapies and to develop safe and effective treatments for those who suffer from schizophrenia.

Chapter 15: The Role of Cognitive Behavioral Therapy in Schizophrenia Treatment

Cognitive behavioral therapy (CBT) is a type of psychotherapy that has been shown to be effective in treating a variety of mental health conditions, including schizophrenia. In this chapter, we will discuss the role of CBT in the treatment of schizophrenia and how it can be used to address the symptoms and challenges of the disorder.

1. What is cognitive behavioral therapy? Cognitive behavioral therapy (CBT) is a type of psychotherapy that aims to change harmful thought patterns and behaviors. CBT is typically short-term and goal-oriented, and it involves identifying and challenging negative thoughts and beliefs and replacing them with more positive, realistic ones.

2. How does CBT work for schizophrenia? In the treatment of schizophrenia, CBT can be used to address specific symptoms, such as

delusions and hallucinations, as well as to improve overall coping skills and functioning. CBT can help people with schizophrenia to identify and challenge negative thought patterns and develop more effective coping strategies.

3. Specific CBT techniques for schizophrenia: There are several specific techniques that may be used in CBT for schizophrenia, including reality testing, cognitive restructuring, and behavioral activation. Reality testing involves helping the person with schizophrenia to evaluate their beliefs and perceptions for accuracy. Cognitive restructuring is recognizing and confronting unfavorable thought patterns and replacing them with more uplifting, realistic ones. Behavioral activation involves encouraging the person with schizophrenia to engage in activities that promote positive mood and functioning.

4. Combining CBT with medication: CBT can be used as a standalone treatment for schizophrenia, but it is often used in combination with medication. When used together, CBT and medication can be very effective in managing symptoms and improving overall functioning.

5. The importance of individualized treatment: It is important to note that every person with schizophrenia is unique, and their treatment should be tailored to their individual needs and circumstances. CBT may not be appropriate for everyone, and other types of psychotherapy or

interventions may be more effective for some individuals.

Cognitive behavioral therapy can be an effective tool in the treatment of schizophrenia, particularly when used in combination with medication and other forms of support. By addressing negative thought patterns and behaviors, CBT can help people with schizophrenia to manage symptoms and improve their quality of life.

Chapter 16: Schizophrenia in Children and Adolescents

Schizophrenia is a mental health disorder that can affect people of all ages, including children and adolescents. It is a serious condition that can make it difficult for young people to think clearly, manage their emotions, and interact with others in a healthy way.

Symptoms of schizophrenia in children and adolescents can include hallucinations, delusions, disorganized thinking and speech, lack of motivation, and difficulty with social interactions. These symptoms can cause a lot of distress and can make it hard for young people to function in their daily lives.

Diagnosing schizophrenia in children and adolescents can be challenging, as the symptoms may be mistaken for other mental health conditions or dismissed as typical teenage behavior. It is important for parents and caregivers to be aware of the signs and to seek professional help if they are concerned about a young person's mental health.

Treatment for schizophrenia in children and adolescents may include medication, therapy, and support from family and mental health professionals. It is important for young people to have a strong support system to help them manage their symptoms and maintain their overall health and well-being.

Living with schizophrenia can be challenging for anyone, but it can be particularly difficult for children and adolescents who are still developing their sense of self and their place in the world. It is important for young people with schizophrenia to have access to resources and support to help them navigate the challenges of the condition and achieve their goals for the future.

Support services, such as vocational and educational support, can also be beneficial for children and adolescents with schizophrenia. These services can help individuals with the illness develop skills to manage their symptoms and live independently.

It is important to note that children and adolescents with schizophrenia can still lead fulfilling lives with proper treatment and support. With a strong support system, many individuals with schizophrenia are able to manage their symptoms and achieve their goals.

Chapter 17: Schizophrenia and Aging

Schizophrenia is a mental disorder that can affect people of all ages, including older adults. As people with schizophrenia age, they may experience changes in symptoms, treatment needs, and social support systems. Healthcare providers and caregivers need to be aware of these changes and provide appropriate care.

One challenge for older adults with schizophrenia is that their symptoms may become more severe or difficult to manage over time. This can be due to a variety of factors, such as changes in brain function, the effects of medication, and the stress of aging. Older adults with schizophrenia may also have other health conditions that can complicate their care, such as diabetes or heart disease.

Another challenge is that older adults with schizophrenia may face social isolation and loneliness. They may have fewer social connections and activities than their peers without schizophrenia, which can contribute to depression and other mental health problems. Caregivers and healthcare providers can help address these issues by encouraging social engagement and providing supportive services.

Treatment for schizophrenia in older adults may involve a combination of medication and therapy, as well as supportive services such as housing assistance and vocational rehabilitation. Healthcare providers need to consider the unique needs of older adults with schizophrenia, including the potential for drug interactions and side effects of medication.

Schizophrenia can be a complex and challenging condition for older adults. However, with appropriate care and support, many older adults with schizophrenia can lead fulfilling lives and maintain their independence. Healthcare providers, caregivers, and families can play an important role in supporting the needs of older adults with schizophrenia and promoting their overall health and well-being.

Chapter 18: Schizophrenia and Employment

Schizophrenia is a mental condition that impairs a person's capacity for clear thinking, feeling, and behavior. It often begins in late adolescence or early adulthood and can impact a person's ability to work and maintain employment.

Employment can play an important role in a person's recovery from schizophrenia, providing structure, routine, and a sense of purpose. However, finding and maintaining employment can be a significant challenge for those living with this condition.

Symptoms of schizophrenia such as delusions, hallucinations, disorganized thinking, and difficulty concentrating can make it difficult for a person to perform job tasks effectively. Social anxiety, depression, and low self-esteem can also impact a person's ability to seek and obtain employment.

There are a variety of treatments and support services available to help individuals with schizophrenia achieve employment goals. Vocational rehabilitation programs can provide job training, career counseling, and job placement assistance. These programs can also help employers understand the unique needs of individuals with schizophrenia and provide workplace accommodations.

It is important for individuals with schizophrenia to communicate with their healthcare provider and support team about their employment goals and any challenges they may face. With appropriate treatment and support, many people with schizophrenia can successfully manage their symptoms and maintain employment.

Chapter 19: Living Well with Schizophrenia

Living with schizophrenia can be challenging, but there are strategies that can help individuals with the disorder improve their quality of life and manage their symptoms. In this chapter, we will explore some of these strategies, including self-care, healthy lifestyle habits, and community involvement.

1. Self-care: Taking care of oneself is important for everyone, but it is especially important for people with schizophrenia. This may include getting enough sleep, eating a healthy diet, staying physically active, and engaging in activities that bring joy and fulfillment. Self-care can also involve practicing relaxation techniques such as deep breathing, meditation, or yoga.

2. Healthy lifestyle habits: In addition to self-care, maintaining healthy lifestyle habits can also be beneficial for people with schizophrenia. This may include avoiding drugs and alcohol, not smoking, and minimizing stress. Research has shown that smoking and drug use can worsen symptoms of schizophrenia, and stress can trigger or exacerbate symptoms.

3. Community involvement: Staying connected to others and engaging in meaningful activities can help

individuals with schizophrenia feel more connected to their communities and improve their sense of well-being. This may involve participating in support groups, volunteering, or pursuing hobbies and interests.

4. Work and education: Many people with schizophrenia are able to work and pursue education, but may require accommodations or support. Vocational training programs and educational institutions can provide resources and support to help individuals with schizophrenia succeed in these areas.

5. Treatment adherence: Consistently taking medication and attending therapy sessions are essential for managing symptoms and preventing relapse. It is important for individuals with schizophrenia to work closely with their healthcare providers to develop a treatment plan that works best for them.

Living with schizophrenia can be challenging, but with the right strategies and support, individuals with the disorder can lead fulfilling and productive lives. In the next chapter, we will discuss some common misconceptions about schizophrenia and how to address them.

Chapter 20: The Importance of Social

Support in Schizophrenia Treatment

Social support is an important component of the treatment plan for schizophrenia. Schizophrenia can be a challenging disorder to manage, and having a strong support system can make a significant difference in the quality of life for people with schizophrenia. In this chapter, we will discuss the importance of social support and the different types of social support available for people with schizophrenia.

1. The importance of social support: Social support can provide a sense of belonging, reduce isolation, and help people with schizophrenia to cope with the challenges of the disorder. Various people and groups, including family, friends, support groups, and mental health professionals, can provide social support.

2. Family support: Family support is an important source of social support for people with schizophrenia. Family members can provide emotional support, and practical assistance, and help to manage medication and appointments. Additionally useful for enhancing communication and lowering stress levels within the family is family therapy.

3. Support groups: Support groups for people with schizophrenia can provide a sense of community and understanding. These groups can be

led by mental health professionals or peer-led and can provide opportunities to share experiences, offer and receive support, and learn coping skills.

4. Mental health professionals: Mental health professionals, such as therapists and case managers, can provide emotional support, counseling, and assistance with medication management and accessing resources. These professionals can also help to connect people with schizophrenia to other sources of social support.

5. Community resources: Community resources, such as vocational rehabilitation programs and housing assistance, can also be helpful sources of social support for people with schizophrenia. These resources can provide practical assistance and help people with schizophrenia to maintain their independence.

By accessing different sources of social support, people with schizophrenia can improve their coping skills, reduce stress, and improve their overall quality of life.

Chapter 21: Supporting Families and Caregivers of People with Schizophrenia

Schizophrenia not only affects the person with the disorder but also their family members and caregivers. It can be challenging to care for someone with schizophrenia, and families and caregivers often need support and resources to help them cope. In this chapter, we will discuss some common challenges faced by families and caregivers of people with schizophrenia, and how to provide support.

1. Coping with the diagnosis: Receiving a diagnosis of schizophrenia can be overwhelming and emotional for both the person with the disorder and their family members. Families and caregivers may experience feelings of guilt, fear, and confusion. It is important to provide emotional support and resources to help families and caregivers cope with the diagnosis.

2. Managing symptoms: Schizophrenia can cause a wide range of symptoms, including hallucinations, delusions, and disorganized thinking. Families and caregivers may struggle with how to manage these symptoms and provide support. It is important to educate families and caregivers about the symptoms of schizophrenia and how to manage them.

3. Providing practical support: People with schizophrenia may have difficulty with daily activities such as cooking, cleaning, and managing finances. Families and caregivers may need to provide practical support to help their loved ones with these tasks. It is important to provide resources and support to help families and caregivers manage these responsibilities.

4. Navigating the healthcare system: The healthcare system can be complex and confusing, and families and caregivers may struggle to navigate it. It is important to provide resources and support to help families and caregivers understand the healthcare system and access appropriate care for their loved ones.

5. Taking care of themselves: Caring for someone with schizophrenia can be emotionally and physically exhausting. Families and caregivers may neglect their own needs in order to care for their loved ones. It is important to encourage families and caregivers to take care of themselves and seek support when needed.

By addressing these challenges and providing support and resources to families and caregivers, we can improve the lives of people with schizophrenia and their loved ones. In the next chapter, we will discuss the role of medication in the treatment of schizophrenia.

Chapter 22: Addressing Misconceptions about Schizophrenia

Schizophrenia is a complex disorder that is often misunderstood by the general public. Misconceptions about the disorder can lead to stigma and discrimination, which can have a negative impact on the lives of people with schizophrenia. In this chapter, we will discuss some common misconceptions about schizophrenia and how to address them.

1. Myth: People with schizophrenia have split personalities.

Fact: Schizophrenia is not the same as multiple personality disorder (now called dissociative identity disorder). People with schizophrenia do not have multiple personalities or split personalities. Instead, schizophrenia is a disorder that affects a person's ability to think, feel, and behave clearly.

2. Myth: People with schizophrenia are violent and dangerous.

Fact: People with schizophrenia are no more likely to be violent than the general population. In actuality, schizophrenia patients are more likely to be attacked than to commit an act of violence. Violence is often the result of other factors such as substance abuse, lack of social support, or a history of trauma.

3. Myth: Schizophrenia is caused by bad parenting or personal weakness.

Fact: Schizophrenia is a brain disorder that is not caused by bad parenting or personal weakness. Although the precise cause of schizophrenia is unknown, a confluence of genetic, environmental, and neurological factors is thought to be responsible.

4. Myth: Schizophrenia is a rare disorder.

Fact: Schizophrenia affects about 1% of the population worldwide. It is not a rare disorder, but it is often misunderstood and underdiagnosed.

5. Myth: Schizophrenia is a lifelong condition with no hope of recovery.

Fact: While schizophrenia is a chronic condition, many people with the disorder are able to manage their symptoms and lead productive lives with the right treatment and support. Treatment may include medication, therapy, and support from family and community resources.

It is important to address these and other misconceptions about schizophrenia in order to reduce stigma and improve the lives of people with the disorder. In the next chapter, we will discuss some common challenges faced by families and caregivers of people with schizophrenia, and how to provide support.

Chapter 23: Future of Schizophrenia Research

Schizophrenia research is a rapidly evolving field, and advances in genetics, epigenetics, and neuroscience are offering new insights into the underlying mechanisms of the disorder. In this chapter, we will explore some of the key areas of research that are likely to shape the future of schizophrenia research.

1. Precision Medicine

One area of research that is likely to become increasingly important in the coming years is precision medicine. Precision medicine involves tailoring treatments to individual patients based on their unique genetic, epigenetic, and environmental profiles. This approach has the potential to greatly improve the efficacy and safety of treatments for schizophrenia, as well as to reduce the risk of side effects.

2. Personalized Risk Prediction

Another area of research that is likely to become increasingly important is personalized risk prediction. Researchers are using large-scale genetic and environmental data to identify individuals who are at increased risk of developing schizophrenia. By identifying these individuals early, it may be possible to intervene before the onset of symptoms, potentially reducing the severity of the disorder.

3. Neuroimaging and Biomarkers

Advances in neuroimaging and biomarker research are also likely to play an important role in the future of schizophrenia research. Researchers are using functional magnetic resonance imaging (fMRI) and other imaging techniques to better understand the neural circuits and systems that are disrupted in schizophrenia. Additionally, biomarkers such as levels of cytokines or inflammatory markers may be used to identify subgroups of patients who may respond better to certain treatments.

4. Psychosocial Interventions

Finally, the role of psychosocial interventions in the treatment of schizophrenia is an area of ongoing research. While antipsychotic medications are the cornerstone of treatment for schizophrenia, psychosocial interventions such as cognitive-behavioral therapy and social skills training may also be effective in reducing symptoms and improving quality of life. Future research will likely continue to explore the potential of these interventions as adjuncts to pharmacotherapy.

Schizophrenia research is a rapidly evolving field, with ongoing advances in genetics, epigenetics, neuroscience, and psychosocial interventions. These advances hold great promise for improving the lives of those who suffer from schizophrenia and offer hope for better treatments and eventual cures for this devastating disorder.

Summary

Schizophrenia is a severe and chronic mental illness that affects approximately 1% of the population worldwide. Recent research has shown that epigenetic modifications, such as DNA methylation and gene expression, may play a key role in its development and progression. Epigenetic biomarkers can be used to identify individuals at high risk for developing schizophrenia or to monitor treatment response. Schizophrenia is a complex disorder with three types of symptoms: positive, negative, and cognitive. Epigenetic therapies could provide a more targeted approach to treating the underlying biological mechanisms of the disorder.

Schizophrenia is a complex disorder that is influenced by genetics, environmental factors, brain development, substance abuse, and stressful life events. Risk factors include genetics, environmental factors, brain development, substance abuse, and stressful life events. DNA methylation is an important epigenetic mechanism that plays a crucial role in regulating gene activity. Studies have found altered DNA methylation patterns in individuals with schizophrenia, suggesting that epigenetic dysregulation may contribute to the development of the disorder. Recent advances in technology and computational methods have provided new tools for investigating these complex interactions.

Recent studies have found that individuals with schizophrenia have altered DNA methylation patterns in several genes involved in neurodevelopment and synaptic plasticity, leading to the development of the disorder. Additionally, prenatal exposure to valproic acid was associated with an increased risk of schizophrenia in offspring. Gene expression is the process by which information stored in DNA is used to produce proteins. Genetic variants associated with an increased risk of schizophrenia have been found to be located in or near genes involved in gene expression.

Schizophrenia is a complex neuropsychiatric disorder that affects 1% of the population worldwide. Recent research has suggested that epigenetic mechanisms, including DNA methylation, may also contribute to the disorder. Studies have identified differential DNA methylation patterns in the brains of individuals with schizophrenia compared to healthy controls. Targeting DNA methylation with drugs such as DNMT inhibitors can improve cognitive and behavioral symptoms in animal models of schizophrenia. Epigenome-wide association studies (EWAS) are a promising avenue of research to identify specific epigenetic modifications associated with schizophrenia.

DNA methylation and gene expression are potential treatment approaches for schizophrenia, but further research is needed to determine their efficacy and safety. Epigenetic-targeted therapies, such as DNA methyltransferase inhibitors, have been shown to improve cognitive function and ameliorate symptoms of schizophrenia in animal models. Schizophrenia is a complex mental disorder that affects millions of people. Recent studies have shown that DNA methylation, a chemical modification that regulates gene expression, may be linked to the development of schizophrenia. Animal models of schizophrenia are used to study the disease in a controlled environment, test potential treatments before they are given to human patients, and provide insights into the basic biological mechanisms of the disorder.

However, animal models may not accurately reflect the genetic and environmental factors that contribute to the disorder in humans. Antipsychotic medications, cognitive-behavioral therapy (CBT), family therapy, support groups, vocational rehabilitation, and housing assistance may be helpful for people with schizophrenia. Epigenetic therapies have the potential to revolutionize the treatment of schizophrenia by targeting specific epigenetic modifications. Challenges include developing therapies specific to epigenetic modifications and long-term safety and efficacy. Cognitive behavioral therapy (CBT) is an effective tool in the treatment of schizophrenia, particularly when used in combination with medication and other forms of support.

Schizophrenia is a mental condition that impairs a person's capacity for clear thinking, feeling, and behavior, and can impact their ability to work and maintain employment. Treatment for schizophrenia in children and adolescents can include medication, therapy, and support from family and mental health professionals. Older adults with schizophrenia may experience changes in symptoms, treatment needs, and social support systems, and healthcare providers and caregivers need to be aware of these changes and provide appropriate care.

The most important details in this chapter are the strategies that can help individuals with schizophrenia improve their quality of life and manage their symptoms. These strategies include self-care, healthy lifestyle habits, and community involvement. Treatment adherence is essential for managing symptoms and preventing relapse. Social support is an important component of the treatment plan for people with schizophrenia. Coping with the diagnosis is a common challenge faced by families and caregivers of people with schizophrenia.

Epigenetic mechanisms, including DNA methylation, may also contribute to schizophrenia. Targeting DNA methylation with drugs such as DNMT inhibitors can improve cognitive and behavioral symptoms in animal models of schizophrenia. Epigenome-wide association studies (EWAS) are a promising avenue of research to identify specific epigenetic modifications associated with schizophrenia. DNA methylation and gene expression are potential treatment approaches for schizophrenia, but further research is needed to determine their efficacy and safety. Epigenetic-targeted therapies, such as DNA methyltransferase inhibitors, have been shown to improve cognitive function and ameliorate symptoms in animal models.

Antipsychotic medications, cognitive-behavioral therapy, family therapy, support groups, vocational rehabilitation, and housing assistance may be helpful for people with schizophrenia. Epigenetic therapies have the potential to revolutionize the treatment of schizophrenia by targeting specific epigenetic modifications. Cognitive behavioral therapy is an effective tool in the treatment of schizophrenia.

Printed in Great Britain
by Amazon

24548751R00040